5/21/04

Pocket Animals

For Pat,
who endows
me with her
caring for my
poems!
Jim

Volumes by James Bertolino:

Pocket Animals, 2002
Snail River, 1995
First Credo, 1986
Precinct Kali & The Gertrude Spicer Story, 1982
New & Selected Poems, 1978
The Alleged Conception, 1976
The Gestures, 1975
Making Space For Our Living, 1975
Employed, 1972

Chapbooks:

Greatest Hits: 1965-2000
26 Poems From Snail River, 2000
Vowel Hollering in a Mob of Consonants, 1997
Goat-Footed Turtle, 1996
Like A Planet, 1994
21 Poems From First Credo, 1992
Are You Tough Enough For the Eighties?, 1979
Terminal Placebos, 1975
Becoming Human, 1970
Stone Marrow, 1969
Day of Change, 1969
Drool, 1968

Pocket Animals

60 Poems by James Bertolino

Egress Studio Press
Bellingham, Washington

Some of these poems were first published in
Bellingham Review, Bluefish, Caprice, Crosscurrents, The Drunken Boat, Duckabush Journal, International Synergy Journal, Jeopardy, La Fusta, Montserrat Review, Poet Lore, The Raven Chronicles, Salt River Review, Wisconsin Review and *Writer's Forum*.

The poems "Pacific Crest" and "Wingbone" were displayed by Seattle's Stonington Gallery, and "The Sixty Poem" was included in the anthology *Family Celebrations*, 1999, Andrews McMeel Publishing.

Published on October 4, 2002 in celebration of the poet's 60th birthday.

ISBN: 0-9725137-0-1
Copyright © 2002 by James Bertolino
Printed in Canada
Cover art and book design by Anita K. Boyle

Egress Studio Press
5581 Noon Road
Bellingham, WA 98226
akboyle@egressstudio.com
www.egressstudio.com

Contents

- 9 The Sixty Poem
- 10 The Hymn
- 11 Kisses
- 12 Pacific Crest
- 13 Wingbone
- 14 Polliwog
- 15 Bamboo
- 16 Foliage
- 17 Hieroglyphs
- 18 Ogre
- 19 Pocket Animal
- 20 Plum
- 21 Weather
- 22 Pucker
- 23 Thought Chemistry
- 24 Beyond Orgasm
- 25 The Swimmer
- 26 Greed
- 27 The Gift
- 28 Zen Mouth
- 29 Asking
- 30 Angel
- 31 Any String
- 32 Impediment
- 33 Grammar
- 34 The Door Opens
- 35 Arms
- 36 His Hands
- 37 Quince
- 38 Fouled

39 *The Liquids*
40 *The Accident*
41 *Lost in Tennessee*
42 *Polkas*
43 *Sabotage*
44 *The Mad*
45 *Chowder*
46 *Her Scent*
47 *The Rose*
48 *At The Bistro*
49 *Elephants*
50 *The Jeweler*
51 *Intellect*
52 *Gestures of Absence*
54 *Grown Men*
55 *Bereft*
56 *Witchcraft*
57 *Mitochondria*
58 *The Estuary*
59 *Apex*
60 *Beak*
61 *Vectors*
62 *Rapture Panic*
63 *Born Again Science*
64 *A Blessing*
65 *Advance*
66 *The Gate*
67 *Order*
68 *Changeling*
69 *Second Coming*

For Anita

The Sixty Poem

Think of sixty nights
and days, sixty riddles
that amaze, sixty thieves of love.

Imagine sixty tons of squash,
sixty daffodils of purple, sixty hillsides
expressing clover.

Wake to sixty doves cooing
to the morning, sixty minnows that leap
the sun, sixty ducks who've dreamed

of platypusses. Taste sixty green
grapes, sixty blue. Sip the juice
of sixty plum-shaped stones.

The Hymn

His breathing increased
and diminshed

the pressure in her room.
She could sense it, the way

the ocean tide, seven forested miles
from the cabin, had seemed to rinse

over him as he lay reading
in the sun.

Kisses

Splash moonlight from the river
onto darkened stones.

When morning comes,
you'll see a broken yolk call the sun

to its yellow nest. Then raindrops, clear
as tiny thoughts of love, spread their bliss

over your face: your mouth
opens to a kiss.

Pacific Crest

You stand high on a ridge
between the shadowed slopes of your past

and the hesitant sun before you. The clouds
are damp threads slipping over and

through your limbs. Now let them draw you cleansed
to the sunlit meadow below, where lupine

beckons with its intoxicating
intervals of blue.

Wingbone

I ask no heaven but this raven's world.
—Richard Nelson

I want to open everything
and pour myself

into the world, but am unable.
So I drip what I've become

through the wingbone of a loon.
Only then do I hear the calling

that mends my heart, that forgives
my distance.

Polliwog

Balanced over the brink of the creek, loose
shred of skin dipping now and then

through ripples: leg of deer.
A bright-eyed black squirrel is interested,

looks away, is interested.
Two dragonflies are sewing taut lines

from oak to fir to blossoming bush.
A polliwog bellies through wet moss.

Bamboo

Her shadow never fragile,
she bends, lies down

like the doe, legs folded.
But under her words, behind

clear eyes, unrest enters with hooves
that splay, nostrils flaring.

Willow, sweet flag, bamboo slick with rain.
Sunlight takes her again.

Foliage

Sandy paths border and give form
to this intricate garden

nestled below the towering stone walls
of a great house. Doves roost here,

and diamond-clear droplets festoon the foliage
which yearns for consumation.

Discipline is a fetish of denial.
Expression the spirit's release.

Hieroglyphs

A rock scarp towers inches over
the debris of pine needles and dried moss,

its surface decorated with lichen hieroglyphs.
Huddled nearby, in an attitude of scholarly respect,

are curved seed pods and cones, exchanging annotations.
A low wind, having discovered a beetle's empty

carapace, sounds a somber note—disturbing
the quiet deciphering of antiquity.

Ogre

She is the scintillant ogre of the biomass,
and there are those whose nostrils widen to danger

when the breeze lifts. But with her a turtle
might find shelter, and perhaps a mouthful

of tasty gnats. When near, even a man
would fill with her loamy musk, would learn her

as she's learned the marshes
and the river.

Pocket Animal

I want to be there to wail
when your feral eyes

blaze. I'd be your pocket animal,
your packet of scat. I'd be fur for your sleep,

huddled close and trembling when wild
with dreams your claws might thrash.

And when it came time to move, I'd take
your scent away on my hooves.

Plum

She bared her plum
blossom bottom

to pee in a brilliant
Mardi Gras

of poison oak, and like
an angel on

the Lord's business,
was unscathed.

Weather

There is a woman whose presence
encloses everything

like weather. He wants to be wet
in her rain. As he thinks this

the cock pheasant's call begins to sound
like sexual moans. His only desire

to do with her body
what air does to a feather.

Pucker

Cradle-shaped wicker chair,
the fine contour of narrow-necked

vase, the smoldering edges
of red dahlias

pucker the air. And you, blue
veins charge your nipples.

Your thoughts reach, hold
like a bowl my space.

Thought Chemistry

*Where love creates the object
        that it loves.* —Darrell Gray

As they move naked across
the room, he says, "Think the perfect

snow." Each cool flake irrefutable,
elegant as it touches skin.

Their damp pores open like mouths
chanting "om." Then everything goes

so still she hears the music blood plays
on his eardrums.

Beyond Orgasm

The space around them
becomes an effigy

of the sensual. They've reached
a region beyond orgasm

where millions of species
are evolving in

a universe where pleasure
is the law.

The Swimmer

Slip into something imagined.

Hover over liquid air, spin,
then anchor your silky boat—

let it rock between pale trees,
let it shiver over the swimmer

growing as he climbs near
what ripples.

When he reaches, take him in.

Greed

He is indulging an honest
greed for real love.

His heart has an ambition known only
to maturity. When he touches,

he wants to reach the body within
her body, the body

that hasn't changed since before
she was born.

The Gift

Their relationship moved forward
like a chrome bar

over the frets
of a guitar—each new stage

of resistance and release
brought music, as though

beyond their ken, some
ghostly hand was strumming.

Zen Mouth

1.

Joseph Campbell tells us
it's a condescension on

the part of the infinite which
allows anyone to exist.

2.

Zen mouth, beginner's
mouth—go to the kiss

that delivers, that shapes
your eternal minutes.

Asking

Please forgive
me if I keep

asking
your name.

Each moment
builds a new universe

and I need to find
you there.

Angel

Being visited
by an angel (in-

visible, subtle) is
like every cell

in your body being
kissed

by this world's
smallest lips.

Any String

Any string
of letters

is a chain that drops
from mind

through sign
into the red-flushed

chambers
of the real.

Impediment

What if God had a speech
impediment

and each time
she spoke

a universe with strange
new laws

would spring into
existence?

Grammar

There are passages where
this universe,

like an ungrammatical
construction, fails

the rules
yet shapes a quirky

beauty, preparing
a new template for life.

The Door Opens

To flutter, a butterfly down
this line to the word bulwark,

or accumulate lightly by moments
like cigarette ash—these are two,

and another is the vowel hollering
in a mob on consonants: thus

the door opens
onto bliss.

Arms

Sometimes she leaves
for the arms

of an idea, or
the idea

of another's arms,
but now, and

always, she
returns.

His Hands

Each time he touches
his new lover

with the same hands that
brutalized his wife

there is a tearing
of his deep webbing

and the dark oil of decay
seeps into his soul.

Quince

Where resinous kisses had drawn her,
she now finds fetid breath.

Before mystery devolved
from luminosity to dull syllables,

her world had tasted
of ginger-spiked honey.

Now love is the metallic wince
of quince dried to sour leather.

Fouled

1.

Not to say fouled, but folded as
the wings of a downed kestrel, as wind

gone from the oxygen bellows
when the family says done.

2.

But if you must, say it: a virtuous idea
may be fouled by prejudices and need

while the heart, fouled by fear, will
howl and destroy what's near.

The Liquids

If we are vessels filled
with all that has been made one

by our love, and if loss is a siphon
drawing away from us what we hold dear,

splashing it back into the world—thus emptied
by grief, do we float higher, do we bob

lightly over this ocean of all
that love has broken?

The Accident

At the last
she clung

to the odor of hot
motor oil,

a dim point
of perception

surrounded by
coma.

Lost in Tennessee

She sensed a wave
of karma gathering

as the plane filled: businessmen
and divorced young women,

a coven of preachers
bound North. She searched

their faces for survivors
and found none.

Polkas

For awhile when I was a child
my father mined ore.

Later mother taught school,
taught mostly girls to make sweet things

for their young men to eat. I can remember
my sister played the saxaphone, both

tenor and alto. Sometimes a little jazz
or dixie came along, but mostly it was polkas.

Sabotage

She realizes how easy
it would be

for the electricians
to sabotage her home, to kill her

while she sleeps,
so she shows them every

courtesy, offers them cookies
and tea.

The Mad

Even the mad have
a favorite flowering bush

in early Spring, a pussycat
whose fur diminishes the world's terror.

A piece of ripe fruit, or new bread still
steaming as the honey is spread,

can bring clear pleasure
to the insane.

Chowder

As he gasped and rattled
I held him, my cat.

When finally his limbs settled
like downy sticks,

something left me, left in my body
a space. And then, as though to cover it,

to close it over, my body
began to shake.

Her Scent

My wife's father died this year.
Last night he called to say

he missed her. He said all he has
is her scent, which smells of forest.

She told me this today, on a hiking trail.
She looked around us at the trees,

the ferns and moss, took a deep breath
and whispered: this is all he has of me.

The Rose

She bends stiffly
from the waist, her

back straight, nose
touching the petals

of a peach-colored
rose. The elusive fragrance

will tell her if she'll live
another day.

At The Bistro

He looked up from reading poetry
to smile at a woman.

She smiled back and
he noticed, as she passed,

her crutches. When she returned
to have a drink with her partner,

one elegant bare leg was missing
below the knee.

Elephants

Near the center of the Book Festival,
creating an island of turbulence

in the nervous herd, and sounding
like two elephant cows

crooning to the little ones, were huddled
the wheelchair poets, palsied of body

and speech, but of love, strong,
of love clear.

The Jeweler

I know a woman who places snake skin
under glass, who would hold

a mountain stream. In her hands a porcupine quill
stitches the world of stone to a dream

of freshwater pearl. The spirits of crystal
and metal gather where light

is her partner. I know a woman
who speaks to bones.

Intellect

After weeks bereft of her muse,
she sits to risk the ritual

of calling poetry down.
She desires the emotional equivalence

of orchids, the equal in spirit to Mount Saint Helens
before the violation, before all she'd known

had been humbled by Nature's
incomprehensible intellect.

Gestures of Absence

1.

What kind of mortgage
will you pay

to live in the palace
of genius?

Will you sacrifice
all you hold dear

to sing purely the haunting
melodies of loss?

2.

When community becomes
another word for triage,

will you ensure the survival of beauty
while children are entitled only

to their deaths? Is leaving and letting
the new way of love? And are gestures

of absence what the last
poets do best?

Grown Men

Out on the street,
I see two grown men

looking into a tree,
then talking quietly,

eyes cast low. I feel concern,
though I know nothing, have

no reason for this emotion
swelling in me.

Bereft

So bereft
of music,

he found an
undermining

ecstasy in
a mosquito

humming
near his ear.

Witchcraft

Pausing
like a dancer

in the garden,
she urinated

over red frills
of lettuce, then filled

a yellow poppy's
cup.

Mitochondria

It has been claimed these
bold little aliens

in each of our cells
are descended from the original

operatives who arrived millions of years ago
to monitor and guide the evolution

of sentience on this
the blue planet.

The Estuary

Our species has reached
the tide-rip

where will and
destiny mingle,

an estuary
balancing the

biosphere
at zero.

Apex

One way reasonably
to conclude

we are the apex
of evolution

is that with us began
the unnatural

and the concept
pollution.

Beak

A beak embedded
in metal

tells
no secrets.

Who will sing
of the yolk?

What law convict
the errant electrons?

Vectors

Reclaiming yellow
vectors, we pull apart

their virus lozenges and
spread them

like sweet paste
over circles of sun-dried

skin. No secret, this is how
we've always won.

Rapture Panic

The born-again Christian, when
her neighbors and friends

begin rising toward heaven,
feels panic, feels the dark

lump of larceny in her heart
grow heavy with gravity,

grow leaden with
its lust for the earth.

Born Again Science

The confluence of science and myth
re-invents the universe.

Long past innocence, we regain
holy participation. Every mote and molecule,

each quantum reaches to complete the ritual
of Second Coming. But when Einstein

broke the nuclear seal,
he also released The Beast.

A Blessing

When at last the dense
darkness opens its indigo heart,

there before you, deep
in a quake-addled

pool of nuclear waste,
you will see

the front parts
of the divine.

Advance

I speak with an uncivil
tongue, and

invite you to advance
for a bruising. Be the planet.

Be the advent of the holoreal,
where nothing

achieves itself
without achieving all.

The Gate

Like two keys
needed to detonate

a bomb, both logic
and intuition

must be engaged
to ease

open the gate
to the New World.

Order

As order in the world diminishes, those
whose routines are complex,

whose feelings and responses tend
toward caricature, will be first

to degenerate to madness.
One now must simplify, streamline

emotion and idea. Speak little, act
less, and only out of stillness.

Changeling

Imagine an entity that resembles
a flock of millions of tiny birds.

This living creature changes shape, speed
and direction with the randomness

of play, of pleasure. It exists in outer space,
its life not limited by feeding, responsibility

or age. Its purpose, simply,
is to change.

Second Coming

Finally your mind goes away,
and in that long instant, that clear

longing, you hear a universe
of musical voices calling to you: come be

with us, please come to us, we've waited.
You know then the sound of your own cells,

and you go to them, forever, so they
will never die.

James Bertolino grew up in
Wisconsin, and has lived in New
York, Ohio, Idaho, Oregon and
Washington—where he teaches
creative writing at Western
Washington University. He
received an MFA in poetry at

Cornell University, and his work has appeared in such
magazines as *Ploughshares, Notre Dame Review, Poetry,
Paris Review, Partisan Review, Another Chicago
Magazine, The Florida Quarterly, Northwest Review,
Seattle Review* and *Wilderness* magazine. His poetry
has been reprinted in over two dozen anthologies,
from publishers in the U.S., as well as England, Italy
and India. Of his nine volumes of poetry, his *Making
Space For Our Living* (Copper Canyon Press) and
Precinct Kali & The Gertude Spicer Story (New Rivers
Press) have been reprinted online by Connecticut
College's Contemporary American Poetry Archive,
and *New & Selected Poems* (Carnegie Mellon), *First
Credo* (Quarterly Review of Literature Award Series)
and *Snail River* (QRL) are still in print. His most
recent chapbooks are *26 Poems From Snail River*
(Egress Studio Press) and *Greatest Hits: 1965-2000*
(Pudding House Publications). He lives outside
Bellingham, Washington on Squalicum Mountain,
beside Toad Lake.